BULLETPOINTS

AIRCRAFT

John Farndon
Consultant: Brian Williams

Miles Kelly
PUBLISHING

First published in 2003 by Miles Kelly Publishing Ltd
Bardfield Centre, Great Bardfield
Essex, CM7 4SL

2 4 6 8 10 9 7 5 3

Project Manager: Ruthie Boardman

Design: Whitelight

Picture Research: Liberty Newton

Assistant: Carol Danenbergs

Production: Estela Godoy

British Library Cataloguing-in-Publication Data
A catalogue record for this book is available from the British Library

ISBN 1-84236-261-5

Printed in China

www.mileskelly.net
info@mileskelly.net

The publishers would like to thank the following artists who have contributed to this book:
Nicholas Forder, Janos Marffy, Terry Riley, Peter Sarson, Mike White

All other pictures are from: MKP archives; Corel;
Digital STOCK; digitalvision; PhotoDisc

Contents

Airships

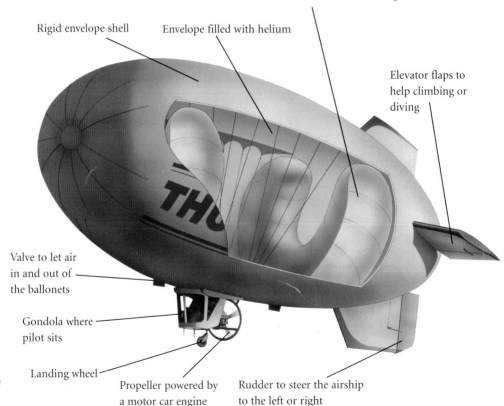

▼ *This is a cutaway of one of the new breed of small airships made from lightweight materials and filled with safe, non-flammable helium gas.*

Airbags or 'ballonets' inside the helium-filled envelope. As the airship climbs, air pressure drops and the helium expands, pushing air out of the ballonets. As the airship drops again, the helium contracts and air is let into the ballonets again

Rigid envelope shell

Envelope filled with helium

Elevator flaps to help climbing or diving

Valve to let air in and out of the ballonets

Gondola where pilot sits

Landing wheel

Propeller powered by a motor car engine

Rudder to steer the airship to the left or right

- **By the mid-1800s** ballooning was a popular activity. In 1852, French engineer Henri Giffard made a cigar-shaped balloon filled with the very light gas hydrogen. He powered it with a steam-driven propeller and added a rudder to make it more 'dirigible' or steerable.

> **FASCINATING FACT**
> Fighter planes could take off from and land on the 1930s airship Akron in mid-air.

- **In 1884** two French inventors, Charles Renard and Arthur Krebs, built the first dirigible balloon, *La France*. This was powered by an electric motor.

- **In 1897** Austrian David Schwartz gave a powered, cigar-shaped balloon a rigid frame to create the first airship.

- **In 1900** Count Ferdinand von Zeppelin built the first of his huge airships, the 128 metre-long LZ-1.

- **In 1909** Zeppelin helped set up the world's first airline, DELAG, flying 148 m long airships, carrying 10,000 passengers in its first four years.

- **In World War I** Germany used Zeppelin airships to scout enemy positions and make the first aerial bombing raids.

- **By the 1920s** vast airships were carrying people to and fro across the Atlantic in the style of a luxury ocean-liner. The *Graf Zeppelin* flew at 130 km/h. In its gondola, 60 or more passengers sat in comfortable lounges, walked to cocktail bars or listened to bands playing.

- **On 6 May 1937** disaster struck the giant 245 m-long airship *Hindenburg* as it docked at Lakehurst, New Jersey. The hydrogen in its balloon caught fire and exploded, killing 35 people. The day of the airship was over.

- **In recent years** there has been a revival of airships for advertising, filled with safer helium gas.

Biplanes

▲ *Felix du Temple built a man-carrying steam-powered monoplane in 1874.*

● **Most early planes** were biplanes (double-wingers) or even triplanes (triple-wingers).

● **Monoplanes** (single-wingers) like Blériot's (see record-breaking flights) were fast and won many early races – because they did not drag on the air like multi-wings.

● **Accidents** by overstressed competition monoplanes made it look as if they were dangerous. Single wings were weak, it seemed, because they had to be very long to give a similar lifting area to multi-wings.

● **In 1912** the French and British banned monoplanes, so all World War I fighter planes were multi-wingers.

▶ *The biplanes of World War I were slow but highly manoeuvrable. Pilots were able to show tremendous flying skill in the first aerial 'dog fights' between planes.*

- **Biplane wings** were strong because struts and wires linked the small, light wings to combine their strength.

- **Famous World War I** fighters included the British Sopwith Camel and Bristol Fighter.

- **The Fokker triplane** flown by German air ace Baron von Richtofen (the Red Baron) was said to be 'fearsome to look at and climbs like a lift'.

- **With their network** of struts and wires, biplanes were affectionately known as 'string bags'.

- **In the years** after World War I, huge biplane airliners were built including the Handley Page Heracles.

- **By the late 1920s** planes could be built strongly all in metal. So to cut drag and boost speed designers went back to monoplanes with planes like the Supermarine S6B. Soon biplanes seemed old-fashioned.

The Wright brothers

▲ *One of the five who witnessed the flight took this picture. But apart from a report in 'Popular Science' the Wrights' success was little known about for five years.*

- **The Wright brothers**, Orville and Wilbur, built the world's first successful plane, the *Flyer*.

- **On 17 December 1903** the Wright brothers made the first powered, long and controlled aeroplane flight at Kitty Hawk, USA.

- **Wilbur Wright** was born in 1867 on a farm near New Castle, Indiana; Orville was born in 1871 in Dayton, Ohio.

- **The Wright brothers** began as bicycle-makers but became keen on flying after hearing about the death of pioneer glider Otto Lilienthal in 1896.

- **From 1899 to 1903** they worked at Kitty Hawk methodically improving their design and flying skill.

- **Many early planes** took off but lacked control. The key to the Wrights' success was stopping the plane rolling, using wires to 'warp' (twist) the wings to lift one side or the other.

- **The *Flyer*'s** wing warp meant it could not only fly level but make balanced, banked turns (like a bicycle cornering).

- **For the first flight** Orville was at the controls.

- **The historic first flight** lasted 12 seconds, in which the *Flyer* travelled 37 m and landed safely.

- **On 5 October 1905** the Wrights flew 38.9 km in 38 minutes.

▶ *Orville and Wilbur Wright's first aeroplane cost less than $1000 to build.*

Bombers of World War II

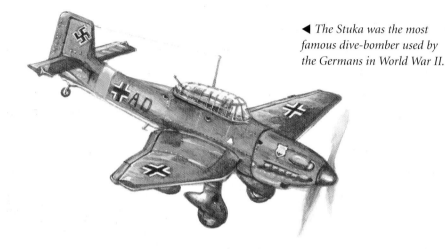

◀ *The Stuka was the most famous dive-bomber used by the Germans in World War II.*

- **In the 1930s** Boeing built the B-17 *Flying Fortress*, bristling with gun turrets to battle its way through to targets even by day.

- **The 1929** Curtis F8C Helldiver was the first 'dive-bomber' – designed to drop its bombs at the end of a long dive on targets like aircraft carriers. German 'Stuka' dive-bombers gained a fearsome name in the German invasions of 1939.

- **The twin-engined** Heinkel III, Dornier Do17 and Junkers Ju88 were the main German bombers in the Blitzkrieg (literally 'lightning war') raids of the Battle of Britain.

- **In December 1939** the heavy loss of British Wellingtons showed that lightly armed bombers could not sustain daylight raids, so the British switched to night raids.

- **Blind-bombing** radar systems like the Hs2, and flare trails left by advance 'Pathfinder' missions, improved accuracy on night raids.

- **The ultra-light** De Havilland Mosquito was fast enough to fly daylight raids.

- **The Russian Ilyushin Il-2** or Stormovik was so good at bombing tanks Stalin said it was 'as necessary to the Red Army as air or bread.'

- **The dambusters** were the Lancasters of 617 squadron of 1943 that attacked German dams with 'bouncing bombs'. These were round bombs designed by Barnes Wallis that bounced over the water surface towards the target dams.

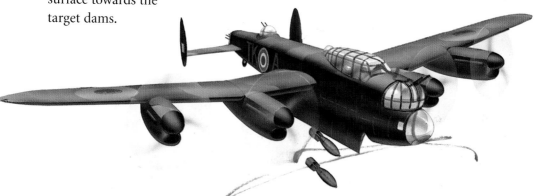

- **Kamikaze** (Japanese for 'divine wind') were fighters loaded with bombs and gasoline which their pilots aimed in suicide dives at enemy ships.

▲ *The British Avro Lancaster could carry 6000 kg of bombs on low altitude raids.*

- **The biggest bomber** was the Boeing B-29 *Superfortress* which could fly over 10,000 m up. In 1945, B-29s dropped atomic bombs on Hiroshima and Nagasaki in Japan.

Fighters of World War II

- **World War II** fighter planes were sleek monoplanes (single-winged aircraft) very different from the biplanes of World War II. Many were developed from racing machines of the 1920s and 1930s.

- **The most famous** British plane was the Supermarine Spitfire. This was developed from the S.6B seaplane which won the coveted Schneider trophy in the late 1920s.

- **The most famous American** fighter was the North American P-51 Mustang, which could reach speeds of over 700 km/h and had a range of 1700 km. It was widely used as an escort for bombers.

- **In the Pacific** US planes like the Grumman Wildcat and Hellcat fought against the fast and highly manoeuvrable Japanese Mitsubishi A6M 'Zero'.

- **The most famous German** fighter was the fast, agile Messerschmitt Bf 109. This was the plane flown by German air ace Erich Hartmann, who shot down 352 enemy planes. Over 33,000 were made during the war.

- **Me 109s** were nicknamed by model. The Bf109E was the Emil. The Bf109G was the Gustav.

- **The German Focke-Wulf** had a big BMW radial engine that enabled it to climb over 1100 km a minute.

- **The most famous Soviet** fighter was the MiG LaGG-3 Interceptor, flown by Soviet air ace Ivan Kozhedub who shot down 62 German planes.

- **The British Hawker Hurricane** was more old-fashioned, slower and less famous than the Spitfire, but its reliability made it highly effective. Hurricanes actually destroyed more enemy aircraft than Spitfires.

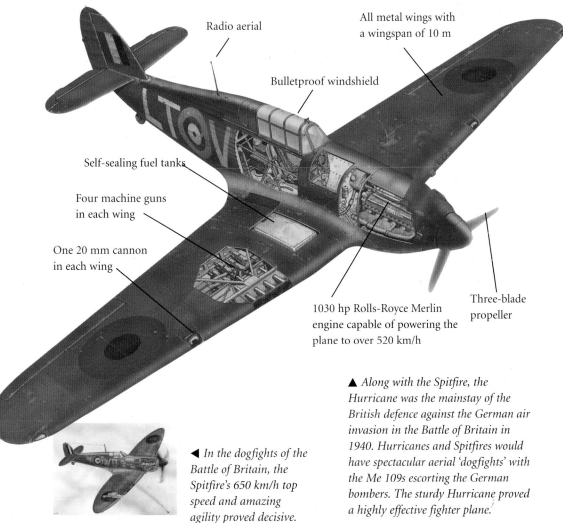

Radio aerial

All metal wings with a wingspan of 10 m

Bulletproof windshield

Self-sealing fuel tanks

Four machine guns in each wing

One 20 mm cannon in each wing

1030 hp Rolls-Royce Merlin engine capable of powering the plane to over 520 km/h

Three-blade propeller

▲ Along with the Spitfire, the Hurricane was the mainstay of the British defence against the German air invasion in the Battle of Britain in 1940. Hurricanes and Spitfires would have spectacular aerial 'dogfights' with the Me 109s escorting the German bombers. The sturdy Hurricane proved a highly effective fighter plane.

◀ In the dogfights of the Battle of Britain, the Spitfire's 650 km/h top speed and amazing agility proved decisive.

13

Warplanes

- **The 870 km/h** German Messerschmitt Me 262 was the first jet fighter. It had straight wings like propeller planes.

- **The Lockheed Shooting Star** was the first successful US jet fighter.

- **The Korean War** of the 1950s saw the first major combat between jet fighters. Most now had swept-back wings, like the Russian MiG-15 and the US F-86 Sabre.

- **In 1954** Boeing introduced the B-52 Superfortress, still the USAF's main bomber because of its huge bomb-carrying capacity.

- **In the 1950s** aircraft began flying close to the ground to avoid detection by radar. On modern ground-hugging planes like the Lockheed F-111 a computer radar system flies the plane automatically at a steady height over hills and valleys. If the system fails, the plane climbs automatically.

▲ *Pilots fly modern jets at supersonic speeds aided by laser-guided weapons, night-vision goggles and other high-tech equipment.*

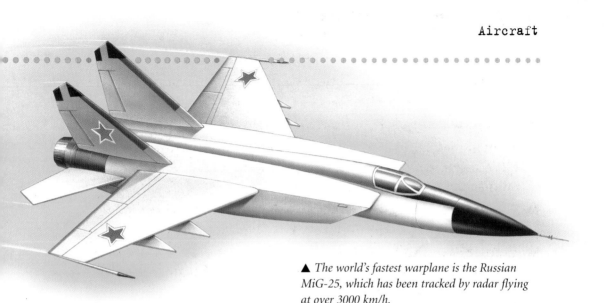

▲ *The world's fastest warplane is the Russian MiG-25, which has been tracked by radar flying at over 3000 km/h.*

- **The Hawker Harrier** of 1968 was the only successful 'jump jet' with swivelling jets for vertical take-off (VTOL).

- **Airborne Early Warning** systems (AEWs) look down from above and detect low-flying aircraft. To evade them the Americans began developing 'stealth' systems like RCS and RAM.

- **RCS** or Radar Cross Section means altering the plane's shape to make it less obvious to radar. RAM (Radar Absorbent Material) is a coating that doesn't reflect radar.

- **In 1988** the US unveiled its first 'stealth' bomber, the B-2, codenamed Have Blue. The F117 stealth fighter followed.

- **The 2500 km/h Russian Sukhoi S-37** Berkut ('golden eagle') of 1997 uses Forward Swept Wings (FSW) for maximum agility, rather than stealth technology.

Taking off

▶ *An F-15 preparing for take-off.*

- **An aircraft's wings** or 'foils' are lifted by the air flowing above and beneath them as they slice through the air.

- **Because the top** of the wing is curved, air pushed over the wing speeds up and stretches out. The stretching of the air reduces its pressure.

- **Underneath the wing** air slows down and bunches up, the air pressure in this area rises.

- **The wing gains 'lift'** as the air around the wing is sucked from above and pushed from below.

- **The amount of lift** depends on the angle of the wing – called the angle of attack – and its shape, and also how fast it is moving through the air.

- **Aircraft** get extra lift for climbing by increasing their speed through the air and by dropping the tail so that the main wings cut through the air at a steeper angle.

- **If the angle of attack** becomes too steep, the airflow breaks up and the wing loses lift. This is called a stall.

- **Planes** take off when air is moving fast enough over the wing to provide enough lift.

- **Airliners** have 'high-lift' slots and flaps on the wings to give extra lift for slow take-off and landing speeds.

... FASCINATING FACT ...
Slots on the wing's leading edge smooth airflow to increase the safe angle of attack.

▲ *The high-lift flaps are down to give extra lift on a climb.*

Controlling a plane

◄ *The controls of planes are so sophisticated that they even allow jets to fly upside down.*

- **A plane** is controlled in the air by moving hinged flaps on its wings and tail.

- **Changing pitch** is when the plane goes nose-up or nose-down to dive or climb.

- **Rolling** is when the plane rolls to one side, dipping one wing or the other.

- **Yawing** refers to when the plane steers to the left or right like a car.

- **Pitch** is controlled by raising or lowering hinged flaps on the rear wings called elevators.

▲ *In old-fashioned planes, the pilot controlled the flaps manually by moving a control stick linked to cables. In modern planes, the flaps are controlled automatically via electric wires (fly-by-wire) or laser beams (fly-by-light). The flight deck of this plane from 30 years ago has lots of dials to help the pilot. Modern planes have 'glass cockpits', which means they have computer screens.*

- **To pitch up** in a small or simple plane, the pilot pulls back on the control column to raise the elevators.

- **Rolling** is controlled by large hinged flaps on the wings called ailerons.

- **To roll left** the pilot pushes the control column to the left, which raises the aileron on the left wing and lowers it on the right.

- **Yawing** is controlled by the vertical hinged flap on the tail called the rudder.

- **To yaw left** the pilot pushes the foot-operated rudder bar forward with his left foot, to swing the rudder left.

Jet engines

- **A kind of jet engine** was built by the Ancient Greek Hero of Alexander in the first century AD. It was a ball driven round by jets of steam escaping from two nozzles.

- **The first jet engines** were built at the same time in the 1930s by Pabst von Ohain in Germany and Frank Whittle in Britain – though neither knew of the other's work.

- **Ohain's engine** was put in the Heinkel HE-178 which first flew on 27 August 1939; Whittle's was put in the Gloster E28 of 1941. The first American jet was the Bell XP-59 Aircomet of 1942.

- **Jets** work by pushing a jet of air out the back. This hits the air so fast that the reaction thrusts the plane forward like a deflating balloon.

- **Jet engines** are also called gas turbines because they burn fuel gas to spin the blades of a turbine non-stop.

- **Turbojets** are the original form of jet engine. Air is scooped in at the front and squeezed by spinning 'compressor' blades. Fuel sprayed into the squeezed air in the middle of the engine burns, making the mixture expand dramatically. The expanding air not only pushes round turbines which drive the compressor, but also sends out a high-speed jet of hot air to propel the plane. This high-speed jet is noisy but good for ultra-fast warplanes and the supersonic Concorde.

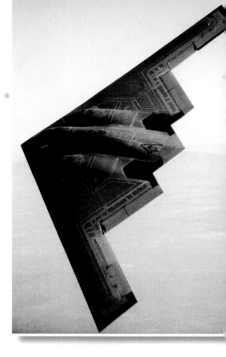

▲ *Like nearly all warplanes today, 'stealth' aircraft are jet-propelled. But the afterburner stream of hot gases from the jets provides a 'signature' that can show up all too clearly on some detection equipment. So stealth aircraft are designed to 'supercruise' – that is, fly at supersonic speeds without much afterburn.*

The engine casing is made of carbon-fibre and plastic honeycomb for lightness. Inside is an outer bypass duct for the 'cold stream' of air from the front fan. An inner duct takes the 'hot stream' through the compressor, combustion chamber and turbine to create the exhaust

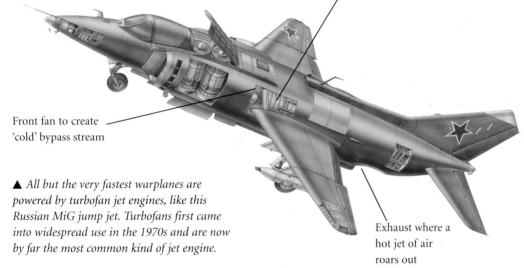

Front fan to create 'cold' bypass stream

▲ *All but the very fastest warplanes are powered by turbofan jet engines, like this Russian MiG jump jet. Turbofans first came into widespread use in the 1970s and are now by far the most common kind of jet engine.*

Exhaust where a hot jet of air roars out

- **Turboprops** are turbojets that use most of their power to turn a propeller rather than force out a hot air jet.

- **Turbofans** are used by most airliners because they are quieter and cheaper to run. In these, extra turbines turn a huge fan at the front. Air driven by this fan bypasses the engine core and gives a huge extra boost at low speeds.

- **Ramjets or** 'flying stovepipes' are the simplest type of jet engine, used only on missiles. They dispense with both compressor and turbine blades and simply rely on the speed of the jet through the air to ram air in through the intake into the engine.

Airliners

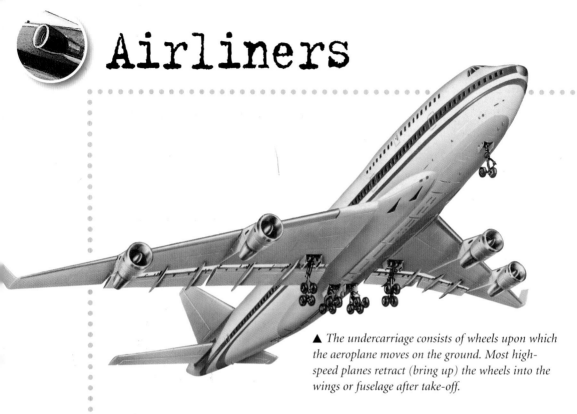

▲ *The undercarriage consists of wheels upon which the aeroplane moves on the ground. Most high-speed planes retract (bring up) the wheels into the wings or fuselage after take-off.*

- **The Boeing 247** of 1933 was the world's first modern airliner, with smooth monoplane wings, streamlined metal body and retractable landing wheels.

- **The Douglas DC-3** of 1936 could carry 21 passengers smoothly at 320 km/h and was the first popular airliner.

- **In 1952** the world's first jet airliner, the De Havilland Comet, came into service.

- **The Comet** more than halved international flight times but several tragic accidents led to its grounding in 1954. It flew again in 1958.

- **The age of jet** air travel really began with the American Boeing 707 and Douglas DC-8 of the late 1950s.

- **The Boeing 747** jumbo jet of 1970 – the first 'wide-bodied jet' – had over 400 seats, making air travel cheap.

- **Four-engined jets** like the 747 can fly 10,000 km non-stop at speeds of 1000 km/h. Two - and three-engined - jets like the DC-10 make shorter flights.

- **Supersonic airliners** able to travel at over 2000 km/h like the Anglo–French Concorde and Russian Tupolev Tu-144 have proved too heavy on fuel and too noisy.

- **The planned 555-seat Airbus** A3XX would be the first double-deck airliner.

> ....**FASCINATING FACT**....
> Spaceplanes like Lockheed–Martin's *Venture Star* may make space trips routine flights.

▲ *The four-engined Boeing 747 flies at 10,000 to 13,000 m – well above most storms – and can fly non-stop from New York to Tokyo.*

23

Airports

- **The world's first airport** was built at Croydon near London in 1928. Many early airports, like Berlin's, were social centres and attracted thousands of intrigued visitors.

- **Before airports** flying boats would land on water. So airports like New York's La Guardia were set close to water to take flying boats.

- **Over 50 airports** around the world now handle over 10 million passengers a year each. Twenty-five of these are in the USA.

- **Six airports** each handle over 30 million passengers, including Chicago's O'Hare and Hong Kong's Chep Lap Kok.

- **The world's largest** airport is King Abdul Aziz in Saudi Arabia. It covers 22,464 hectares. The USA's biggest is Dallas. Europe's biggest is Paris's Charles de Gaulle.

- **Hong Kong's** Chep Lap Kok airport, opened in 1998, is one of the world's most modern.

- **Kansai** airport in Japan is built entirely on an artificial island in Osaka Bay so that it can operate 24 hours a day, without disturbing people with noise.

- **In early airports** terminals for each flight were set in a line, as at Kansas and Munich. But as flights increased, this layout meant passengers had a long way to walk.

- **Terminals in the 1970s** were set in extending piers like Amsterdam's Schiphol, or satellites like Los Angeles.

- **New airport terminals** like London's Stansted are set apart and linked by electric cars called 'people-movers'.

▶ *In the 1970s, Boeing 747 jumbo jets needed runways 4 km long to take-off, but better performance means they now need less.*

Rockets

- **Rockets** work by burning fuel. As fuel burns and swells out behind, the swelling pushes the rocket forward.

- **Solid-fuel rockets** are the oldest of all engines, used by the Chinese a thousand years ago.

- **Solid-fuel engines** are basically rods of solid, rubbery fuel with a tube down the middle.

- **Solid-fuel rockets** are usually only used for model rockets and small booster rockets. But the Space Shuttle has two solid-fuel rocket boosters (SRBs) as well as three main liquid-fuel engines.

- **Most powerful launch rockets** use liquid fuel. The Shuttle uses hydrogen. Other fuels include kerosene.

▶ *The mighty Atlas Rocket was used to launch America's first astronauts into space.*

- **Liquid fuel** only burns with oxygen, so rockets must also carry an oxidizer (a substance that gives oxygen) such as liquid oxygen (LOX) or nitrogen tetroxide.

- **Future rocket drives** include nuclear thermal engines that would use a nuclear reactor to heat the gas blasted out.

- **NASA's Deep Space-1** project is based on xenon ion engines which thrust electrically charged particles called ions, not hot gases, out of the back of the craft.

- **Solar thermal engines** of the future would collect the Sun's rays with a large mirror to heat gases.

▶ *Only powerful rockets can give the thrust to overcome gravity and launch spacecraft into space. They fall away in three stages once the spacecraft is travelling fast enough.*

Missiles

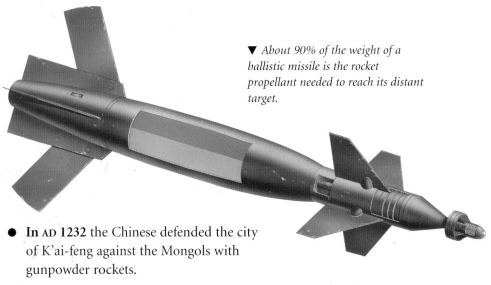

▼ *About 90% of the weight of a ballistic missile is the rocket propellant needed to reach its distant target.*

- **In AD 1232** the Chinese defended the city of K'ai-feng against the Mongols with gunpowder rockets.

- **In the early 1800s** British army officer William Congreve developed metal rockets carrying explosives.

- **In World War II** the Germans developed the first guided missiles – missiles steered to their target in flight.

- **The most frightening** German guided missiles were the V-1 flying bombs or 'doodlebugs' and the V-2 supersonic rockets. The V-2s flew at 5300 km/h.

- **Ballistic missiles** arch through the air like a thrown ball. Rockets propel them on the upward trajectory (path). They then coast down on their target. Cruise missiles are propelled by jet on a low flat path all the way.

- **In the 1950s** the USA and Soviet Union competed to develop long-range ICBMs (Intercontinental Ballistic Missiles) usually armed with nuclear warheads.

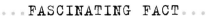

FASCINATING FACT
American Tomahawk cruise missiles could
be aimed through goalposts at both ends
of a football field 500 km away.

- **In the 1960s** antiballistic
  missiles were developed to
  shoot down missiles.

- **Some ICBMs** have a range of
  over 5000 km. Short-range
  missiles (SRBMs) like
  Pershings reach up to 500 km.

- **SAMs** (surface-to-air missiles)
  like Redeye are fired from the
  ground at aircraft. Some can
  be fired by a soldier with a
  backpack. AAMs (air-to-air
  missiles) like Sidewinders are
  fired from planes for use
  against other planes.

▶ *Rocket missiles can carry nuclear
warheads or other weapons halfway
around the world.*

Supersonic planes

- **Supersonic planes** travel faster than the speed of sound.

- **The speed of sound** is about 1220 km/h at sea level at 15°C.

- **Sound travels** slower higher up, so the speed of sound is about 1060 km/h at 12,000 m.

- **Supersonic** plane speeds are given in Mach numbers. These are the speed of the plane divided by the speed of sound at the plane's altitude.

- **A plane flying** at 1500 km/h at 12,000 m, where the speed of sound is 1060 km/h, is at Mach 1.46.

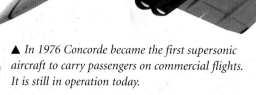

- **A plane flying** at supersonic speeds builds up shock waves in front and behind because it keeps catching up and compressing the sound waves in front of it.

- **The double shock waves** create a sharp crack called a sonic boom that is heard on the ground. Two booms can often be heard one or two seconds apart.

▲ *In 1976 Concorde became the first supersonic aircraft to carry passengers on commercial flights. It is still in operation today.*

- **In 1947** Chuck Yeager of the USAF made the first supersonic flight in the Bell X-1 rocket plane. The X-15 rocket plane later reached speeds faster than Mach 6. Speeds faster than Mach 5 are called hypersonic.
- **The first jet plane** to fly supersonic was the F-100 Super Sabre fighter of 1953. The first supersonic bomber was the USAF's Convair B-58 Hustler first used in 1956.

▼ *Supersonic jet fighter planes are used by the military to intercept and attack enemy aircraft.*

...**FASCINATING FACT**...
Spaceplanes of the near future may
reach speeds of Mach 15.

Record-breaking flights

- **On 25 July 1909** Louis Blériot made the first flight across the English Channel in a plane he built himself.
- **On 8–31 May 1919** (with stops) Capt A.C. Read and his crew made the first flight across the Atlantic in a Curtiss flying boat.
- **On 14–15 June 1919** John Alcock and Arthur Brown made the first non-stop flight across the Atlantic in an open cockpit Vickers Vimy biplane.
- **On 12 November–10 December 1921** brothers Keith and Ross Smith made the first flight from England to Australia.
- **In February 1921** William Corey was the first person to fly solo across the United States.
- **In 1927** Frenchman Louis Breguet made the first flight across the South Atlantic.

▼ *Alcock and Brown's flight from Newfoundland to Ireland took 15 hours 57 minutes for the 1950-mile journey.*

> ···**FASCINATING FACT**···
>
> In December 1986, the American plane *Voyager*, piloted by Dick Rutan and Jeana Yeager, flew round the world non-stop in nine days.

▲ *Louis Bleriot's first flight across the English Channel in 1909.*

- **On 21 May 1927** American Charles Lindbergh made the first solo flight across the Atlantic in the *Spirit of St Louis*.

- **In July 1931** Wiley Post made the fastest round-the-world flight yet.

- **The story of Post's epic flight** was recorded in the book *Round the World in Eight Days*.

Helicopters

Without a tail rotor, the helicopter would spin round the opposite way to the main rotors. This is called torque reaction. The tail rotor also acts as a rudder to swing the tail left or right

To fly up or down, the pilot alters the angle or 'pitch' of the main rotor blades with the 'collective pitch' control. When the blades cut through the air almost flat, they give no lift and the helicopter sinks. To climb, the pilot steepens the pitch to increase lift

The angle of the blades is changed via rods linked to a sliding collar round the rotor shaft, called the swashplate

To fly forwards or back, or for a banked turn, the pilot tilts the whole rotor with the 'cyclic pitch' control

Rockets

Tail rotor drive shaft

Engine

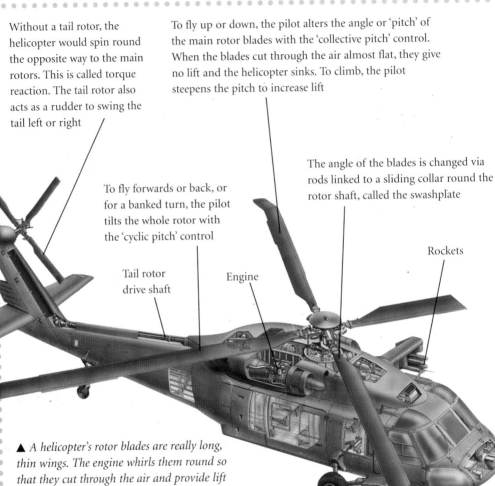

▲ *A helicopter's rotor blades are really long, thin wings. The engine whirls them round so that they cut through the air and provide lift just like conventional wings (see taking off). But they are also like propellers, hauling the helicopter up just as a propeller pulls a plane.*

Stabilizers

- **Toy helicopters** have been around for centuries, and those made by air pioneer Sir George Cayley in the early 19th century are the most famous.

- **On 13 November 1907** a primitive helicopter with two sets of rotors lifted French mechanic Paul Cornu off the ground for 20 seconds.

- **The problem** with pioneer helicopters was control. The key was to vary the pitch of the rotor blades.

- **In 1937** German designer Heinrich Focke built an aircraft with two huge variable pitch rotors instead of wings and achieved a controlled hover. Months later, German Anton Flettner built the first true helicopter.

- **Focke and Flettner's** machines had two rotors turning in opposite directions to prevent torque reaction. In 1939, Russian-born American Igor Sikorsky solved the problem by adding a tail rotor.

- **The Jesus nut** that holds the main rotor to the shaft got its name because pilots said, "Oh Jesus, if that nut comes off...".

- **The biggest helicopter** was the Russian Mil Mi-12 Homer of 1968 which could lift 40,204 kg up to 2255 m.

- **The fastest helicopter** is the Westland Lynx, which flew at 402 km/h on 6 August 1986.

- **The Boeing/Sikorsky RAH-66** Comanche unveiled in 1999 is the first helicopter using stealth technology (see warplanes). It is made of carbon-fibre and other composite materials, and the rotor hub is hidden.

▶ *The Vietnam War saw the rise of heavily armed helicopter gunships designed to hit targets such as tanks.*

Balloons

- **Balloons** are bags filled with a light gas or hot air – both so light that the balloon floats in the air.

- **Balloons** designed to carry people into the air are of two types: hot-air balloons and gas balloons filled with hydrogen or helium.

- **Hot-air balloons** have a burner that continually fills the balloon with warm air to keep it afloat.

- **To carry two people** a hot-air balloon must have a bag of about 1700 cubic metres in volume.

- **Balloons** are normally launched at dusk or dawn when the air is quite calm.

◄ *Hot-air ballooning has become a popular sport since Ed Yost, Tracy Barnes and other Americans began to make the bags from polyester in the 1960s.*

- **As the air in the bag cools** the balloon gradually sinks. To maintain height, the balloonist lights the burner to add warm air again.

- **To descend quickly** the balloonist pulls a cord to let air out through a vent in the top of the bag.

- **The first flight** in a hot-air balloon was made in Paris on 15 October 1783 by French scientist Jean de Rozier in a balloon made by the Montgolfier brothers.

- **The first hydrogen gas balloon flight** was made in Paris on 1 December 1783 by Jacques Charles and one of the two brothers Robert who built the balloon.

- **On 20 March 1999** Swiss Bertran Piccard and British Brian Jones completed the first round-the-world hot-air balloon flight.

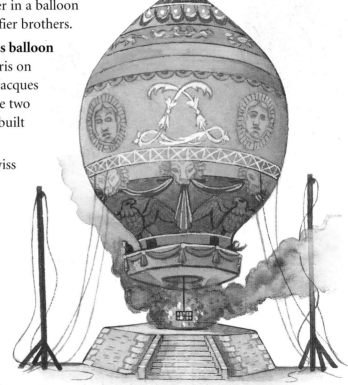

▶ *The Montgolfier balloon was built from paper and silk.*

Autogiros and microlights

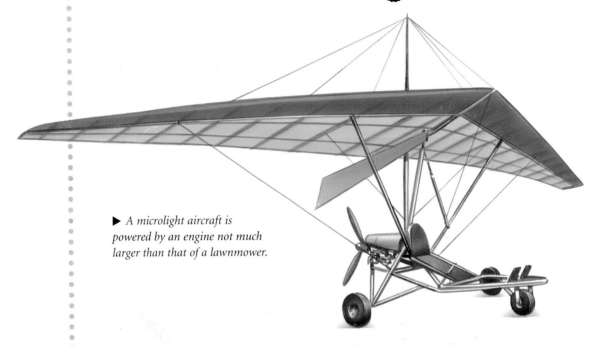

▶ *A microlight aircraft is powered by an engine not much larger than that of a lawnmower.*

- **In the 1400s** many European children played with flying toys kept aloft by whirling blades.

- **The autogiro** was built in 1923 by the Spanish inventor Juan de la Cierva.

- **An autogiro** is lifted, not by wings, but by turning rotor blades.

- **A helicopter uses** a powerful motor to turn the rotors; an autogiro's rotors are turned round by the pressure of air as the plane flies forward.

- **The autogiro** is pulled forward by propeller blades on the front like an ordinary small plane.

- **The autogiro** can fly at up to 225 km/h, but cannot hover like a helicopter.

- **In the USA and Australia** microlights are called ultralights. They are small, very light aircraft.

- **The first microlight** was a hang-glider with a chainsaw motor, built by American hang-glider pioneer Bill Bennett in 1973.

- **Some microlights** have flexible fabric wings like hang-gliders.

- **Some microlights** have fixed wings with control flaps to steer them in flight.

▲ *For a while in the 1930s, many people believed autogiros would be the Model T Fords of the air – aircraft for everyone.*

Index